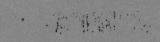

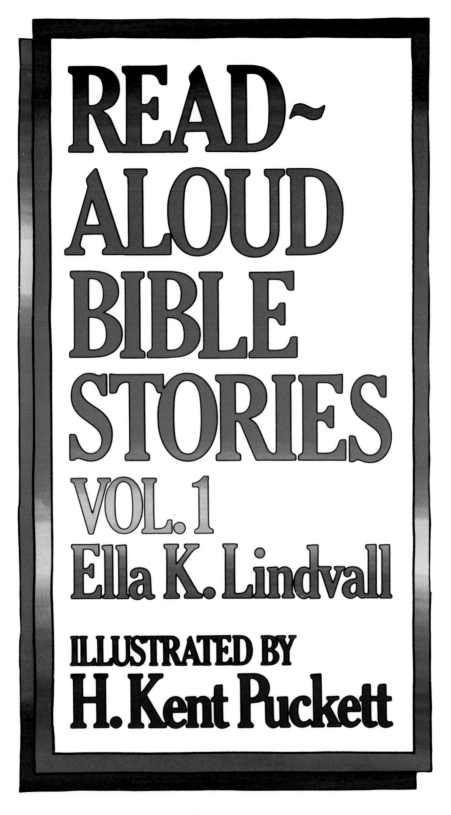

READ~ ALOUD BIBLE STORIES

VOL. 1

Ella K. Lindvall

ILLUSTRATED BY
H. Kent Puckett

MOODY PUBLISHERS
CHICAGO

For Jason

Library of Congress Cataloging in Publication Data

Lindvall, Ella K.
    Real aloud Bible stories

    Contents: v. 1. The man who was too little.
The man who couldn't see. The boys and girls
and Jesus. The wind that obeyed. The man
who said, "thank you."
    1. Bible stories, English. [1. Bible stories—
N. T.] Title.
BS551.2.L48   220.9 505   82-2114

ISBN-13: 978-0-8024-7163-5 (v. 1)
ISBN-13: 978-0-8024-7164-2 (v. 2)
ISBN-13: 978-0-8024-7165-9 (v. 3)
ISBN-13: 978-0-8024-7166-6 (v. 4)
ISBN-13: 978-0-8024-1264-5 (v. 5)

Printed by Versa Press in East Peoria, IL., July, 2021

We hope you enjoy this book from Moody Publishers.
Our goal is to provide high-quality, thought-provoking
books and products that connect truth to your real needs
and challenges. For more information on other books and
products written and produced from a biblical perspective,
go to www.moodypublishers.com or write to:

Moody Publishers
820 N. LaSalle Boulevard
Chicago, IL 60610

37 39 40 38 36

Printed in the United States of America

Contents

The Man Who Was Too Little
(Luke 19: 1-10)

Zaccheus was too little.
He was too little
to reach high things.
He was too little
to see over big things.

And one day Zaccheus almost didn't get to see Jesus because he was TOO LITTLE.

"Jesus is coming
down the street,"
somebody said.
"Let's go out to see Him."

Now Zaccheus wanted
to see what Jesus looked like.
So when other people
hurried outside,
Zaccheus hurried, too.

The little street
was full of
daddies and mommies
and grandpas and grandmas
and uncles and aunts
and boys and girls
and friends—
all wanting to see Jesus.

"Here He comes!"
a man shouted.
"Here comes Jesus now.
I see Him!
I see Him!"

Zaccheus tried to see, too.
First he looked this way.
Then he looked that way.

But there were
too many people,
and Zaccheus was
TOO LITTLE.
He couldn't see Jesus
at all.

What shall I do?
Zaccheus thought.
I know.
I'll run and climb
the big tree.
THEN I can see Him.

Too-little Zaccheus
started to run.
(Go, Zaccheus. Go fast.)
He came to the tree.
(Climb, Zaccheus. Climb fast.)

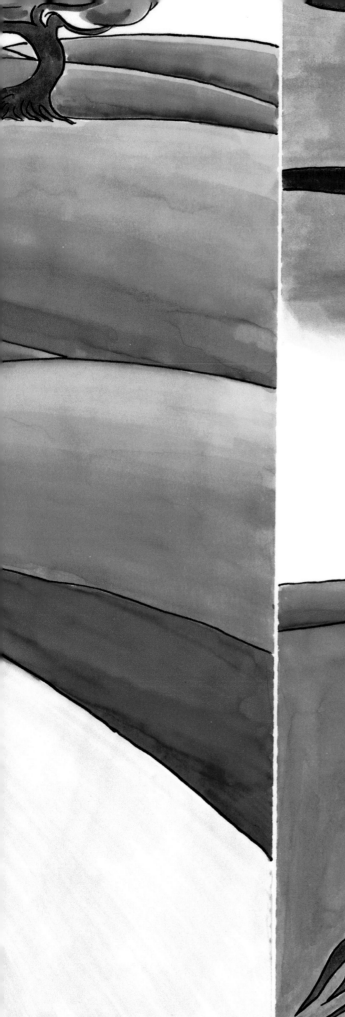

Now Zaccheus
was up high.
He could see
the daddies coming.
And the mommies.
And the grandpas.
And the grandmas.
And the uncles.
And the aunts.
And the boys.
And the girls.
And the friends.
And THEN—

ZACCHEUS SAW JESUS.

Jesus stopped at the big tree.
He looked up—
right at Zaccheus.
"Zaccheus," He said, "hurry.
Come down. I'm coming
to your house."

Well, too-little Zaccheus
did hurry.
He went down
that tree fast.
And then HAPPY ZACCHEUS
took Jesus home
for dinner.

What did you learn?

Jesus knew Zaccheus
was in that tree.
He even knew Zaccheus's name.
Jesus knows where you are—
all the time.
He knows your name, too.

The Man Who Couldn't See
(Mark 10: 46-52; Luke 18:35-43)

Poor Bartimaeus.
His eyes were sick.

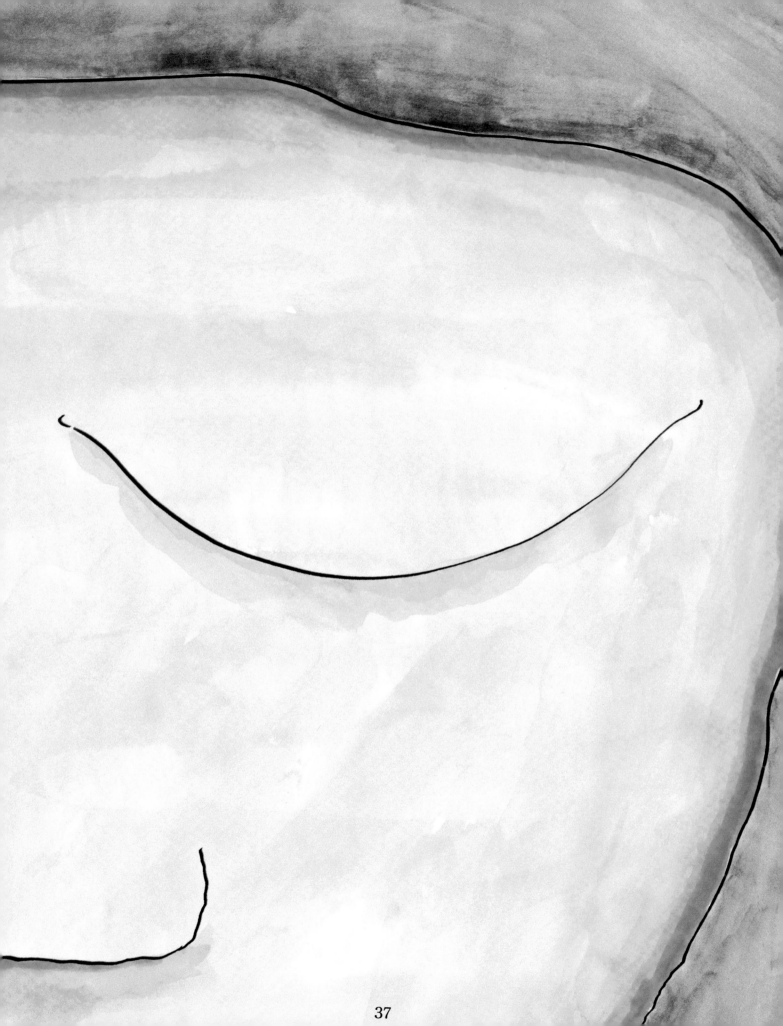

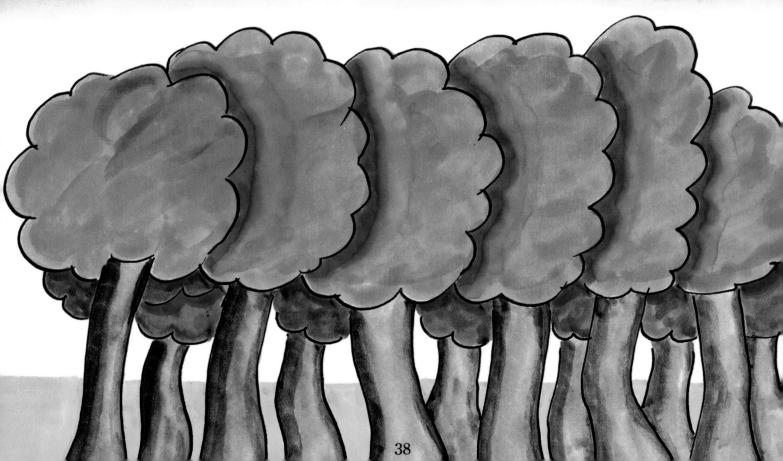

He couldn't see the sun.

He couldn't see the trees.

He couldn't see the houses.

He couldn't see people.
But Bartimaeus could hear.
And one day —

He heard lots of people walking.
Step. Step. Step.
He heard lots of people talking.
Talk. Talk. Talk.

"What is happening?" asked Bartimaeus. "What is happening?"

"It's Jesus," somebody said.
"Jesus is coming down the road.
We're all walking with Him."

It's Jesus, Bartimaeus said to himself. *Jesus can make my eyes well.*

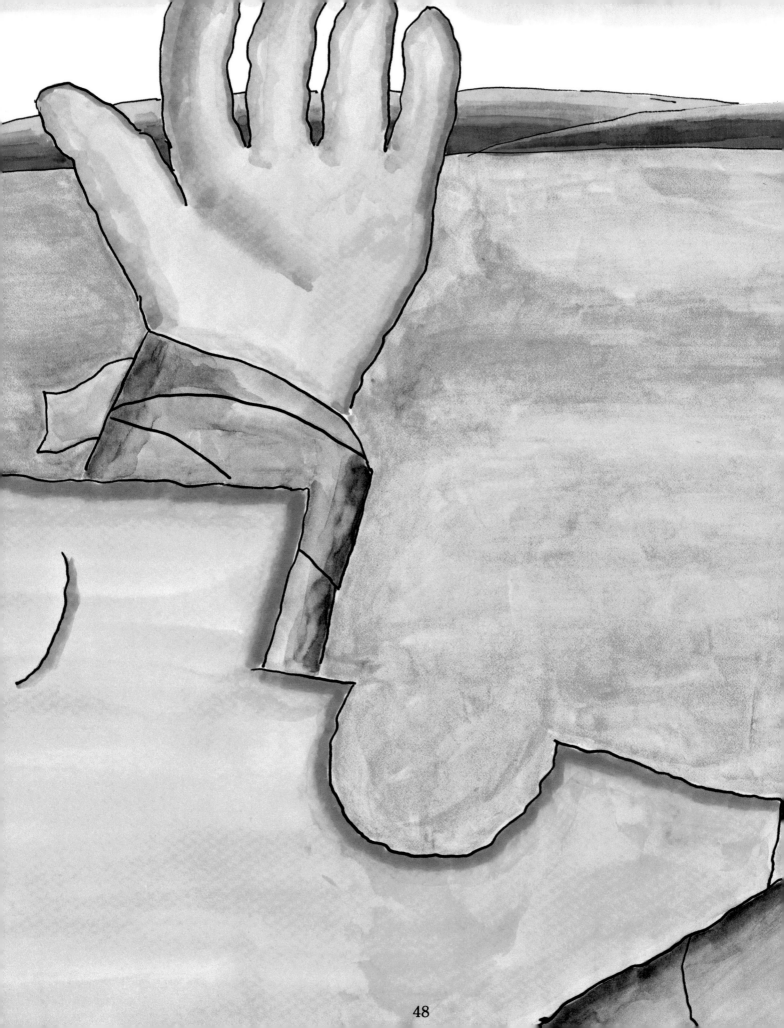

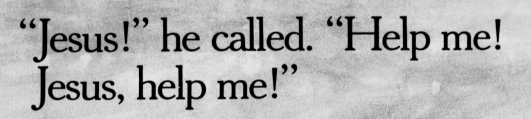

"Jesus!" he called. "Help me!
Jesus, help me!"

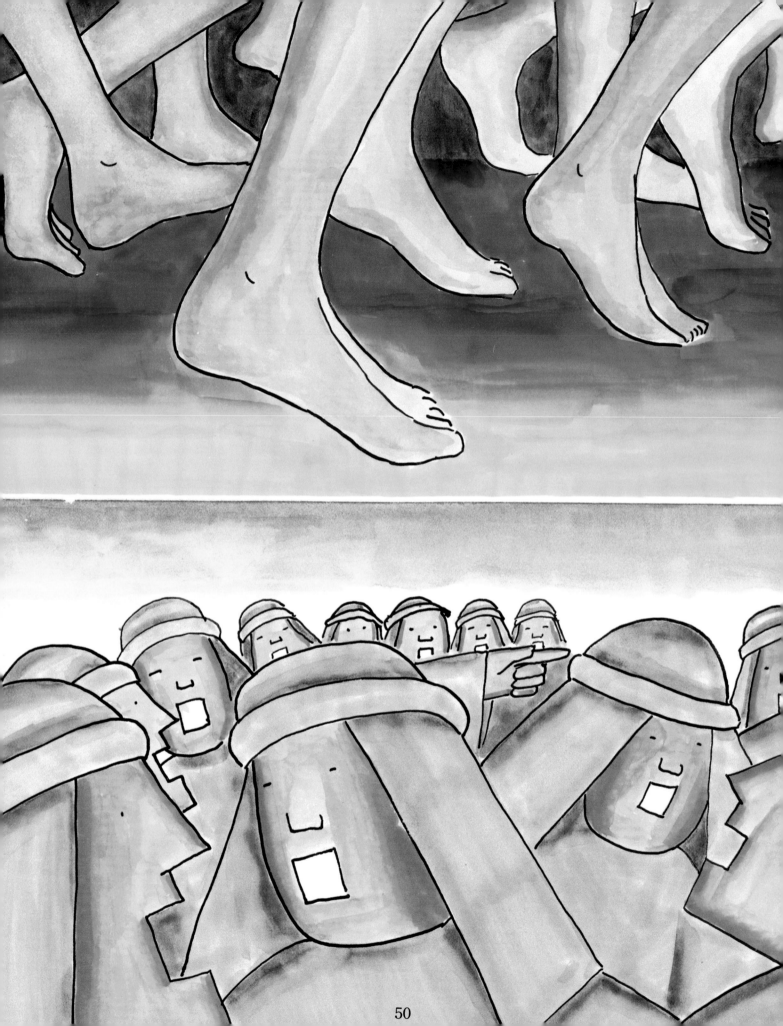

Now, lots of people were making noise walking.

Lots of people were making noise talking. BUT—

JESUS HEARD BARTIMAEUS
ANYWAY,
and Jesus stood still.
"What do you want me to do
for you?" He asked kindly.

"Lord," said Bartimaeus,
"I want to see again."
What do you think Jesus said?

I'll tell you what Jesus said.
He said yes.
"You may see," He told Bartimaeus.
And all at once—

Bartimaeus saw the sun.
Bartimaeus saw the trees.

Bartimaeus saw the houses.
Bartimaeus saw the people.
But best of all —

Bartimaeus saw Jesus.

What did you learn?

Jesus hears when people
talk to Him.
He heard Bartimaeus.
When you talk to Jesus,
He hears you, too.

The Boys and Girls and Jesus
(Matthew 19: 13-15; Mark 10: 13-16; Luke 18: 15-17)

Every day Jesus was busy.
He made sick eyes see.
He made sick legs walk.

Every day Jesus was busy.
He talked to people.
He told people
how good God is.

Every day lots of
daddies and mommies came
to hear Jesus talk.
Grandpas and grandmas
and friends came, too.
Some days—

there were too many people
to get inside a house.
Then, the daddies
and the mommies
and the grandpas
and the grandmas
and the friends

73

stood right out
in the sunshine
and listened
to what Jesus said.

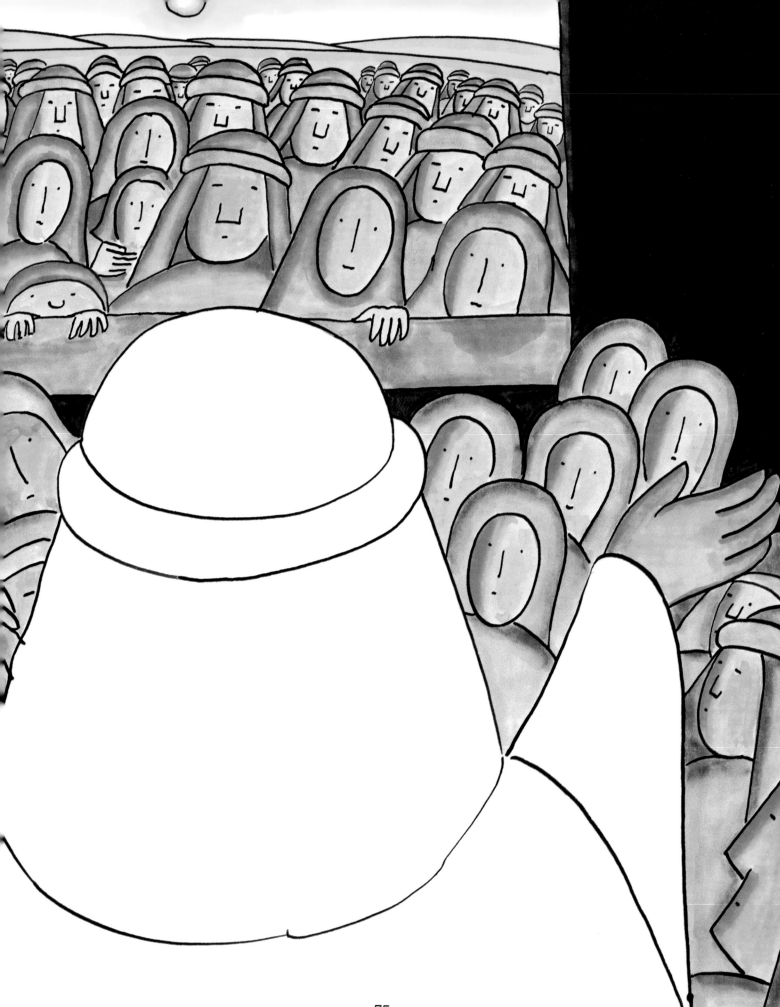

One day somebody asked,
"Do you think Jesus
would put His hands
on our boys and girls
and pray for them?
Do you think He would?"

Somebody else said,
"YES, *I* think He would."
So down the street they went —

the daddies
and the mommies
and the grandpas
and the grandmas
and their boys and girls—
on the way to Jesus.

Jesus' friends
saw them coming.
Jesus' friends said, "NO.
Don't bring children
to Jesus.
He is TOO BUSY."

83

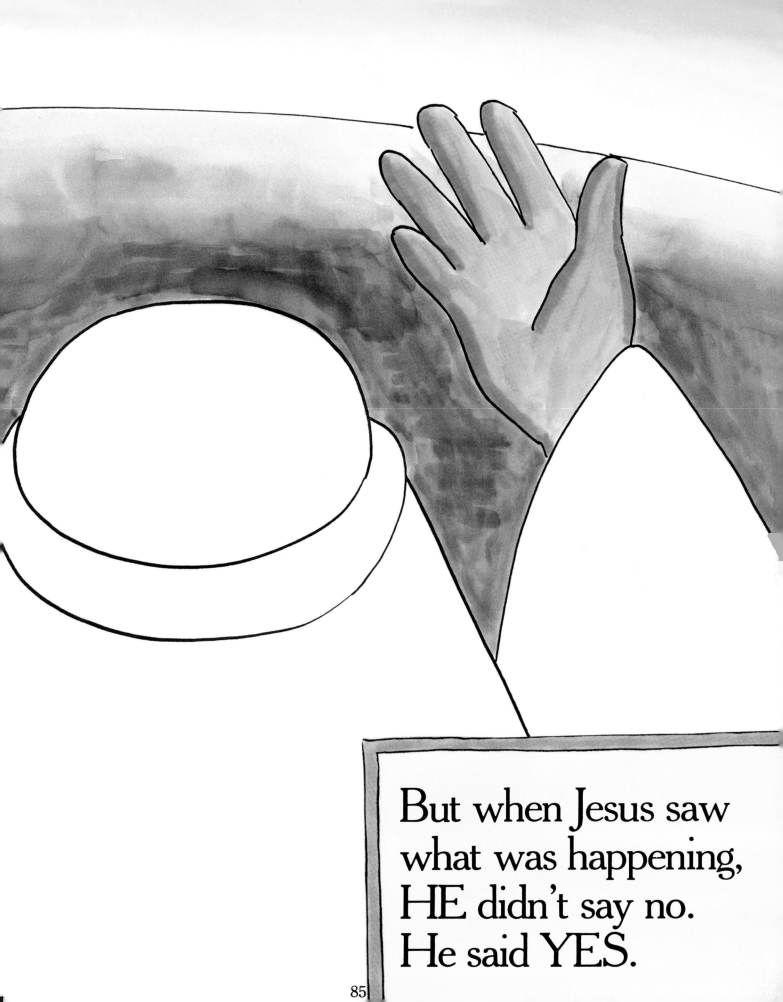

But when Jesus saw
what was happening,
HE didn't say no.
He said YES.

"Let the little children come to Me," He said. Then Jesus reached down. He picked up the boys and girls one by one.

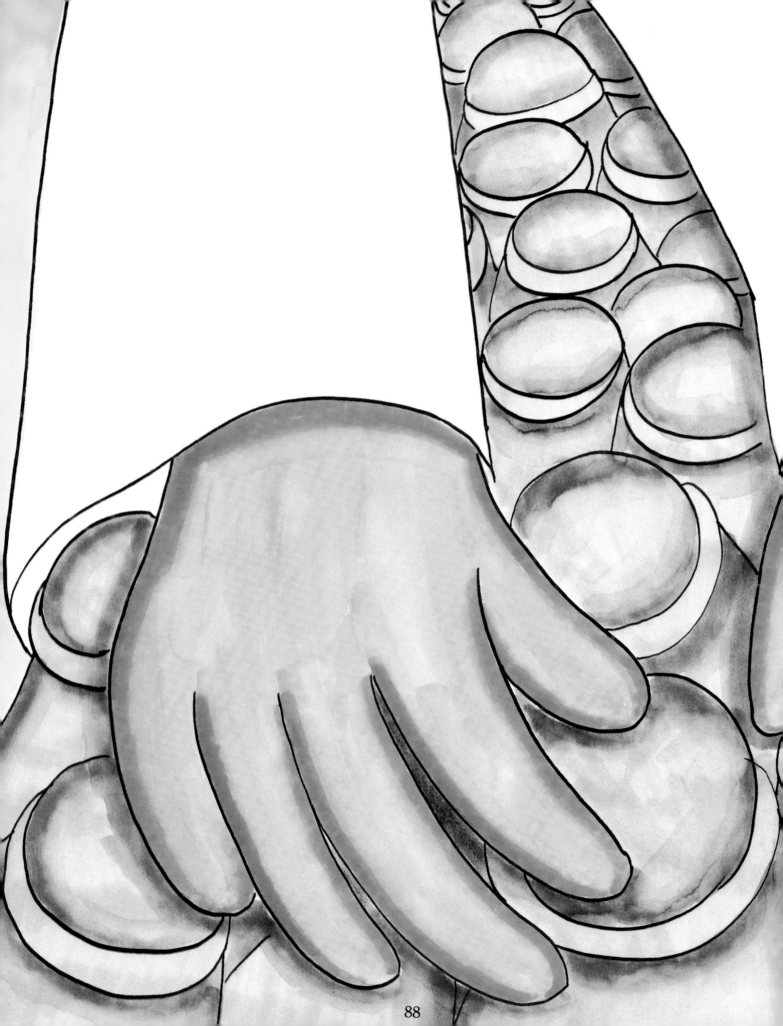

He put His arms
around them
and loved them.
He put His hands on them
and prayed.

Jesus' friends thought,
*Oh. Jesus is NOT
too busy for
boys and girls.
He loves them.*

After the children
had all been on Jesus' lap,
the daddies
and the mommies
and the grandpas
and the grandmas
took them home.

What did you learn?

Jesus loves boys.
Jesus loves girls.
Jesus loves _____ (child's name)
very much.

The Wind That Obeyed
(Matthew 8:23-27; Mark 4: 35-41; Luke 8: 22-25)

"Come," said Jesus.
"Get into the boat.
Let's go for a ride."

Jesus got into the boat.
Jesus' friends
got into the boat.
Splash went the
little waves.
Splash. Splash.

Jesus' friends began to make the boat go. *Pull, push, pull, push.*

But Jesus was tired.
He lay down
in the back of the boat
and went to sleep.

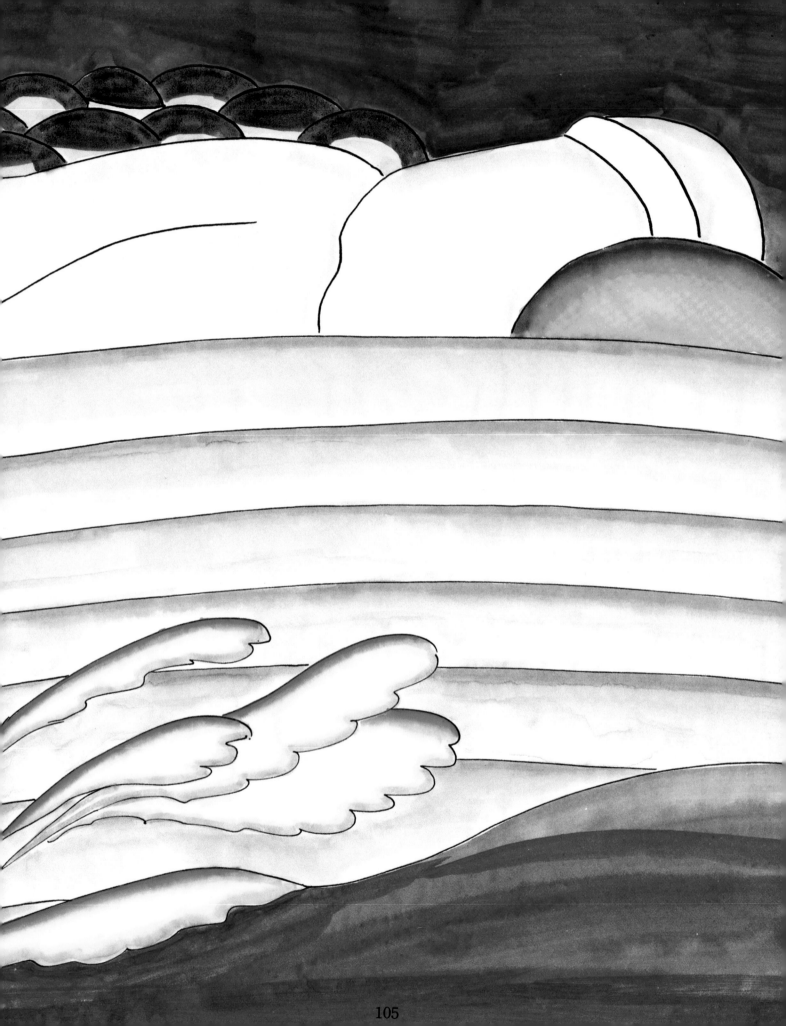

Now, while the boat
was going,
the wind started to blow.
Who-o-o.
Who-o-o.
Who-o-o.

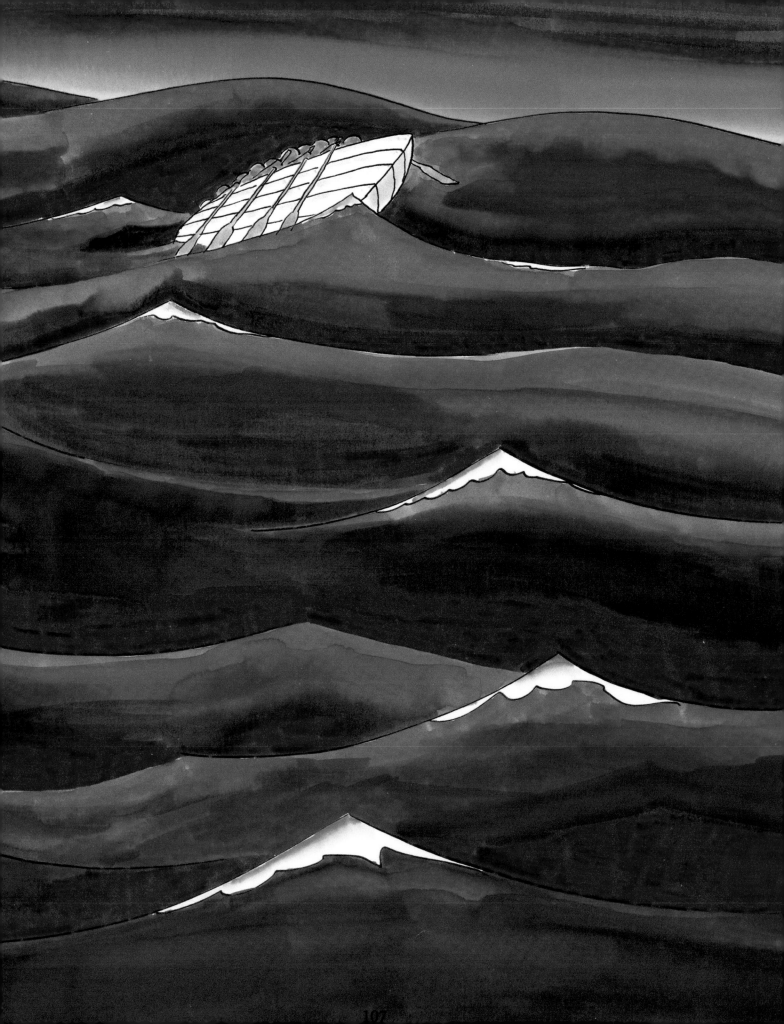

It blew the men's hair.
It blew their clothes.
It blew the water.
WHO-O-O!

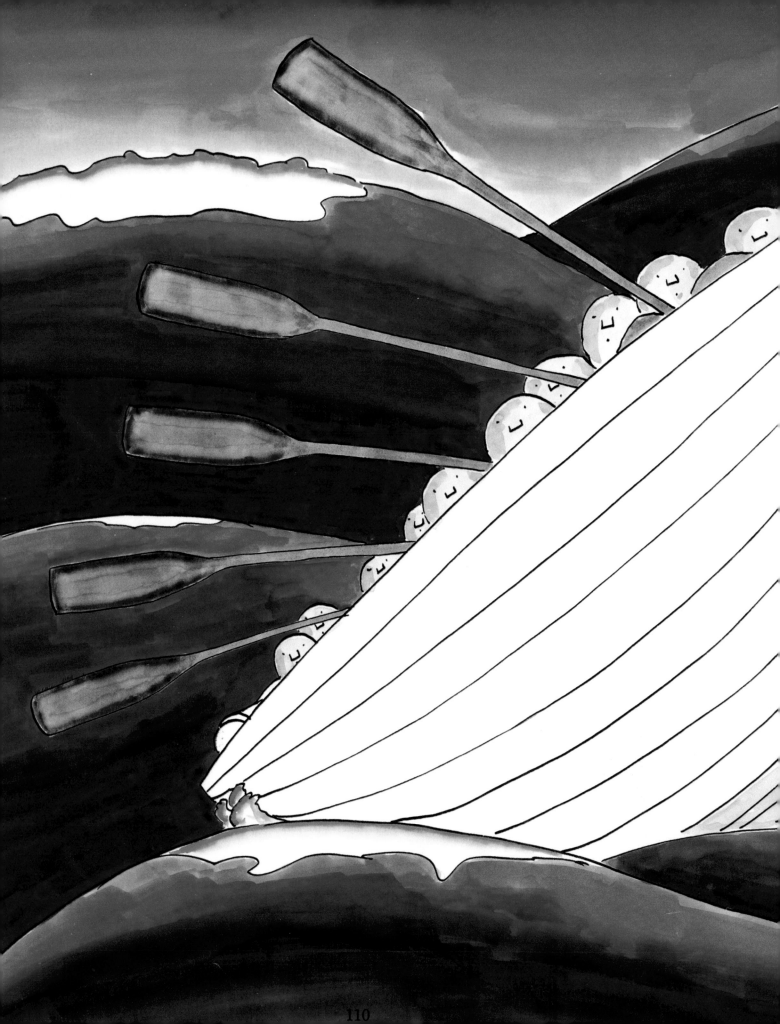

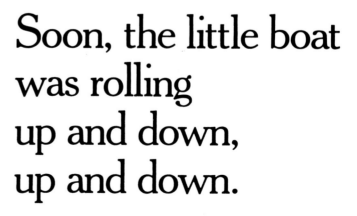

Soon, the little boat
was rolling
up and down,
up and down.

111

Then some water
came into the boat.
SPLASH! went the big waves.
SPLASH! SPLASH!
Jesus' friends were wet.
They were afraid, too.

"Let's tell Jesus,"
they said.
"Save us, Lord!
Wake up!
Wake up!"

Jesus opened His eyes.
He saw the water splash.
He heard the wind blow.
But He said, "Why are
you afraid? I'm here."

Then Jesus talked
to the wind.
He talked to the water.
He said, "Sshhh. Be still."
And do you know
what happened?

The wind stopped
blowing.
The water stopped
splashing.
They both got still
as still could be.

Jesus' friends
looked around.
Everything was
quiet and safe.
"Who IS Jesus?"
they said.
"Even the wind
and the water
do what He says."

I know who Jesus is.
Do you?
Jesus made the wind.
Jesus made the water.
Jesus is God.

What did you learn?
Jesus took care of His friends.
Jesus is God.
He can take care of you, too.

The Man Who Said, "Thank You"
(Luke 17: 11-19)

One, two, three,
four, five, six,
seven, eight, nine,
ten men were very sick.
They were so sick
the doctor couldn't
make them better.

They were so sick
they couldn't stay
with their mommies
and daddies or
boys and girls.
They had to stay outside
by themselves.

All of them
wanted to be well
so they could go home.

One day
the ten sick men saw
lots of people
coming up the road.

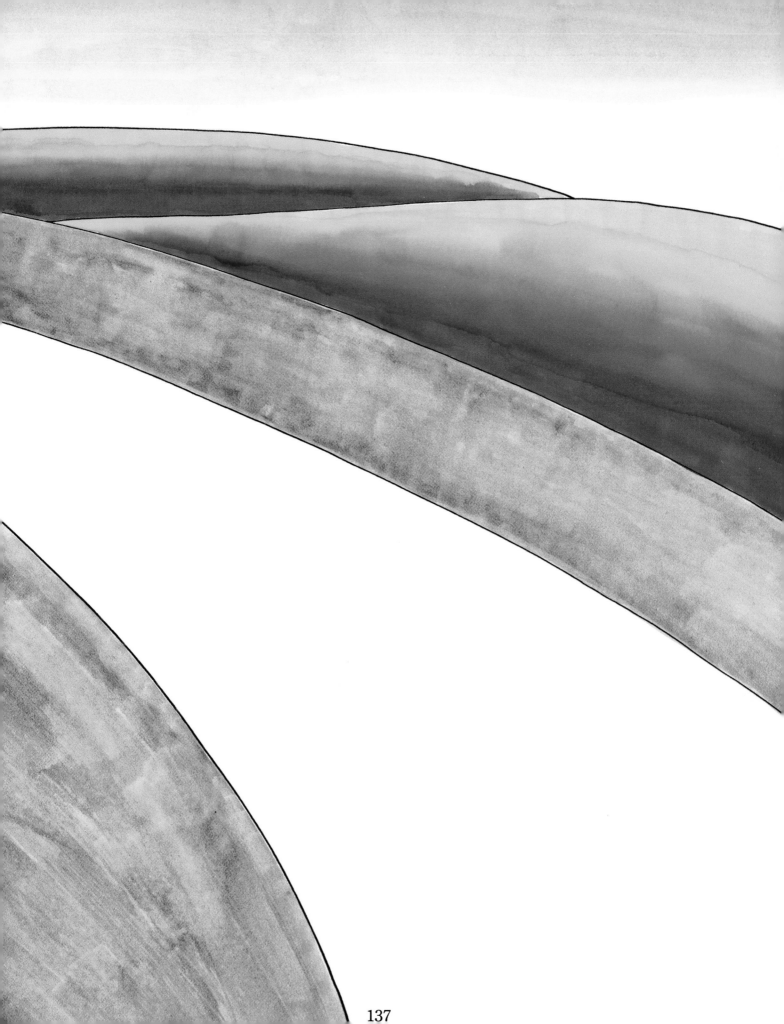

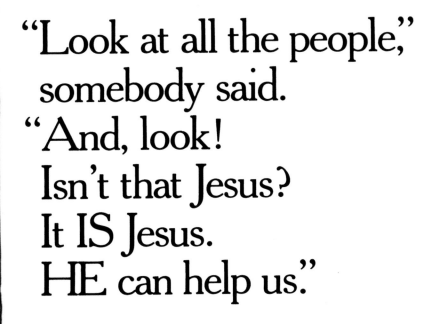

"Look at all the people,"
somebody said.
"And, look!
Isn't that Jesus?
It IS Jesus.
HE can help us."

Jesus was far away,
so the men yelled
in big voices,
"JESUS, HELP US!
JESUS, HELP US!"

Now, Jesus knows everything.
He knew what they wanted.
Right away,
He called back,

143

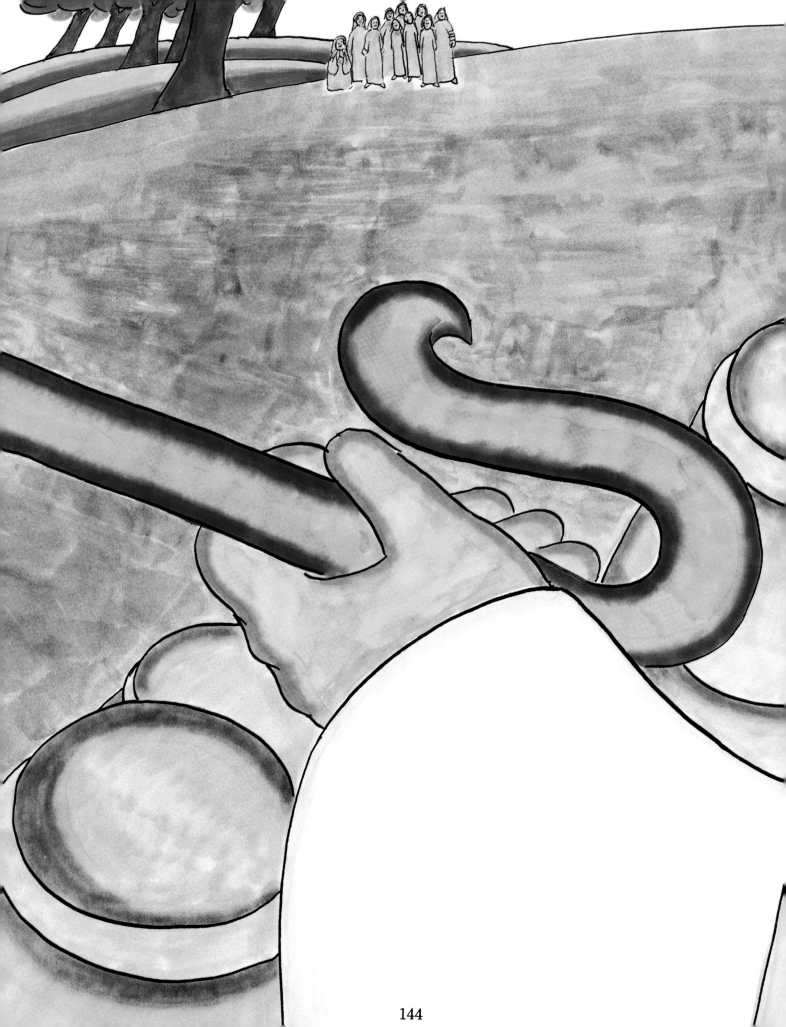

"Go to the men
who work in
God's Temple-church.
Let them see if
you are still sick."

I'm glad to tell you the men did just what Jesus said.
One, two, three, four, five, six, seven, eight, nine, ten sick men started down the road.
Step, step, step.
Step, step, step.

All at once
somebody said,
"Oh, my hands—they're better!"
Another man said,
"My arms—they're better!"

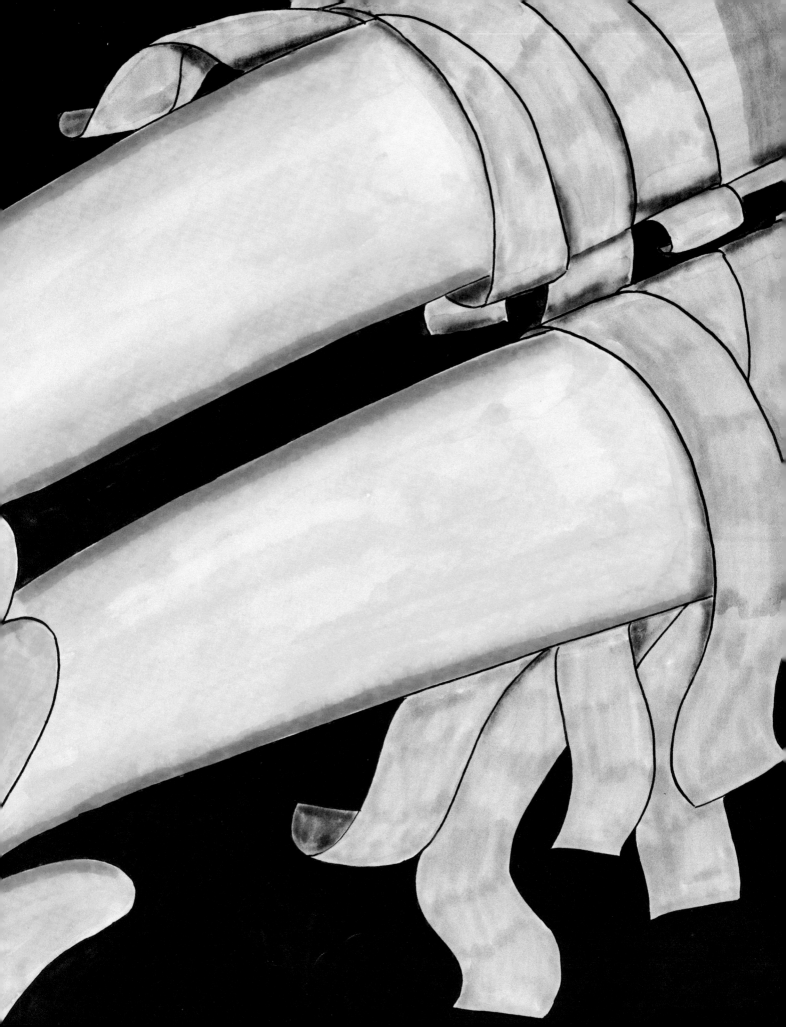

Somebody else shouted,
"Jesus has made us well.
NOW WE CAN GO HOME."
And away they hurried—
one, two, three,
four, five, six,
seven, eight, nine men.
Just nine.

One man didn't
hurry home.
That man wanted
to say, "Thank You,"
first.
He ran back to Jesus.

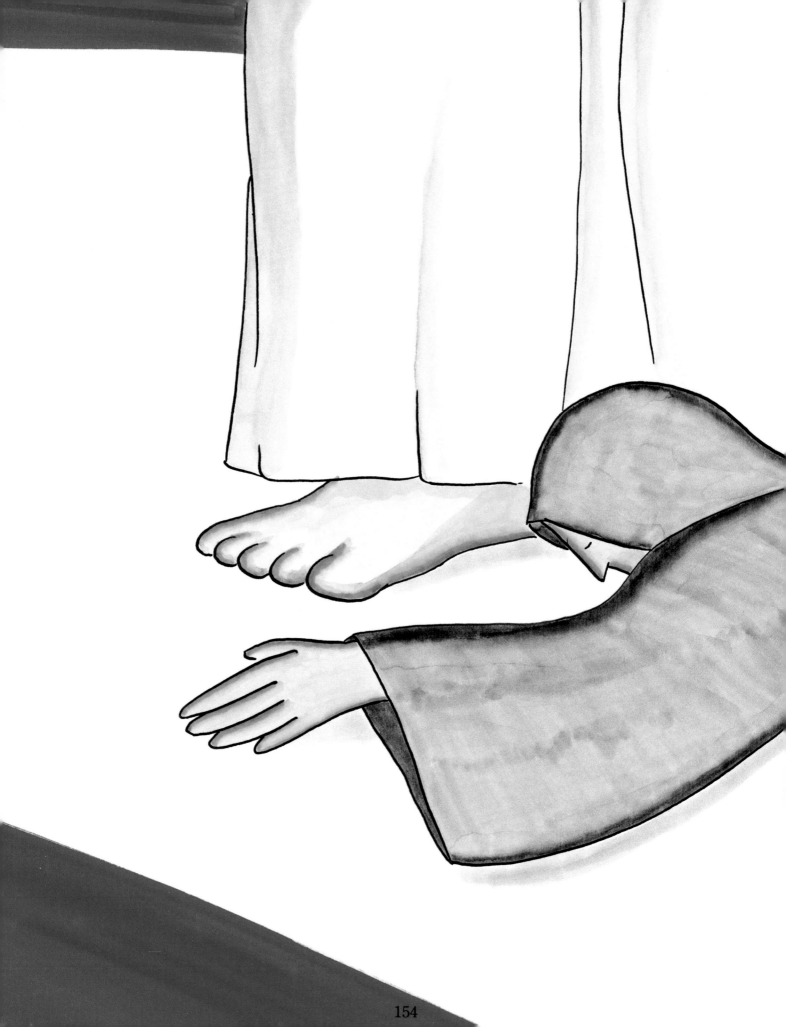

"Thank God!"
the man shouted.
"I'm well!
Thank You,"
he said to Jesus.
"Thank You.
Thank You."

Jesus was pleased.
But He was sad, too.
"Didn't I make
ten men well?" He asked.
"Did only one man
come back to say, 'Thank You'?"
Then He told the man
he could go home.

What did you learn?
Jesus was pleased
when the man
thanked Him.
Jesus is pleased
when YOU tell Him,
"Thank You."
What could you
thank Jesus for
right now?